T0040010

Blackbird

David Harrower's plays include *Knives in Hens* (Traverse, 1995), *Kill the Old, Torture Their Young* (Traverse, 1998), *Presence* (Royal Court, 2001), *Dark Earth* (Traverse, 2003). Adaptations/versions include *The Chrysalids* (NT Connections, 1996), *Six Characters in Search of an Author* (Young Vic, 2001), *Woyzeck* (Edinburgh Lyceum, 2001), *Ivanov* (National Theatre, 2002), *The Girl on the Sofa* (Edinburgh International Festival/Schaubühne, 2002) and *Tales from the Vienna Woods* (National Theatre, 2003). *Blackbird* was shortlisted for the Saltire Society Book of the Year Award, 2005 and was awarded the Lawrence Olivier Award for best new play in 2007.

by the same author

DARK EARTH
PRESENCE
THE CHRYSALIDS
(adapted from the novel by John Wyndham)
PURPLE
(translated from the play by Jon Fosse
and included in *Shell Connections 2003* anthology)
TALES FROM THE VIENNA WOODS (Horváth)

Published by Methuen
KNIVES IN HENS
KILL THE OLD, TORTURE THEIR YOUNG
SIX CHARACTERS IN SEARCH OF AN AUTHOR (Pirandello)

Published by Oberon
IVANOV (Chekhov)
THE GIRL ON THE SOFA (Jon Fosse)

DAVID HARROWER

Blackbird

FARRAR, STRAUS AND GIROUX

NEW YORK

Farrar, Straus and Giroux
175 Varick Street, New York 10014

Copyright © 2005 by David Harrower
All rights reserved
Printed in the United States of America
This edition originally published in 2006 by Faber and Faber Limited,
Great Britain
Published in the United States by Farrar, Straus and Giroux
First American edition, 2007

Library of Congress Control Number: 2006365887
Paperback ISBN: 978-0-571-23319-9

Our books may be purchased in bulk for promotional, educational,
or business use. Please contact your local bookseller or the
Macmillan Corporate and Premium Sales Department at
1-800-221-7945, extension 5442, or by e-mail at
MacmillanSpecialMarkets@macmillan.com.

www.fsgbooks.com
www.twitter.com/fsgbooks • www.facebook.com/fsgbooks

P1

CAUTION: All rights whatsoever in this work, amateur or professional,
are strictly reserved. Applications for permission for any use
whatsoever must be made in advance, before rehearsals begin,
to Casarotto Ramsey Limited, Waverley House,
7-12 Noel Street, London W1F 8GQ. No performance
may be given unless a license has first been obtained.

For Selma

Acknowledgements

This play was written while I was the Edinburgh
International Festival Creative Fellow 2004 at the
Institute for the Advanced Studies in the Humanities
at Edinburgh University.

My thanks to Brian McMaster, Director of the EIF,
and at IASH the former Director, John Frow,
Anthea Taylor and Donald Ferguson
and all the Fellows I met during my time there.

Blackbird was commissioned by the Edinburgh International Festival and was first presented in the King's Theatre, Edinburgh, on 15 August 2005. The production transferred to the Albery Theatre, London, from 7 February 2006, where it was produced by Michael Edwards and Carole Winter for MJE Productions. The cast was as follows:

Una Jodhi May
Ray Roger Allam

Director Peter Stein
Set Designer Ferdinand Wögerbauer
Costume Designer Moidele Bickel
Lighting Designer Japhy Weideman
Composer Arturo Annecchino
Sound Ferdinando Nicci
Associate Director David Salter

Una, late twenties. Coat, dress, gloves; carries a bag.
Ray, mid-fifties. Trousers, shirt, tie; a mobile phone
clipped to his belt.

In a room in which there's a low table, several chairs,
several lockers. The door is closed.

A swing-top bin, full of litter.

On the floor, around the chairs, more abandoned litter –
food packaging mostly, with bits of food still visible.

An oblong frosted window through which passing figures
can occasionally be seen.

Una   Shock.

Ray   Of course.
Yes.
Now

Pause.

Una   And

Ray   Wait.

Pause.

He goes to the closed door, opens it a small way.

Una   You were busy.

Ray   Yes.

Una   They

Ray   I still am busy.

I was with one of the
our managers.
We're in the middle of something.
They
So I might
I will be sent for.
I will get called away.
I'm still needed.

Una   Don't people have homes?

Ray   Homes?

Una   Outside.

Ray   I don't

Una   To go to.
Homes to go to.
They're still working.
It's late.

Ray   We're finishing soon.
They'll be going soon.
An order came in delayed and
of course
but we have to process it no matter how late.
And late is
The time's not a consideration.
We have to process the order and then dispatch it.
It's a very quick turnaround.

Una   Do they go home when you tell them?

Ray   No.
But I, I make sure all is
when the work's done.
I have to make sure.

Una   But so what do you actually make here?

Ray It's
     Dentistry.

Una Because

Ray Sometimes pharmaceutical.

Una The name on the front.
     You can't tell.
     Like one of those low buildings you pass
     I passed
     on the motorway, on the way here.
     Low buildings, always one-storey, and you you
     Cars parked outside
     no clue what's happening *in*side.
     Only a digital clock thing on the outside telling
        what the temperature is.
     This is like that.
     The barrier at the gate.

     Ray's begun to pick up some of the rubbish.

     This is where you eat?

Ray No.
     Not in here.
     Not me.
     The staff do.

Una They shouldn't leave it like this.
     The floor.

     He takes the rubbish to the bin.

     It's too full.

     He crams it into the bin.

     Where do you eat?

Ray Are you on your own?

Una Yes.
     You mean alone?

3

Ray	Yes.
	By yourself.
Una	Yes.
Ray	Can you tell me why you're here?
	What've you come here for?
Una	Do they get breaks?
	Fag breaks?
	Will any of them
Ray	No.
	Too late now.
Una	We won't be interrupted?
	I don't want people walking in here.
Ray	What is there to interrupt?
	What are you wanting?
	I haven't much time.
Una	I saw
Ray	And to be honest I
Una	What?
Ray	I
	I don't *have* to be in here with you.
	You know that, don't you?
	You're aware of that?
	I don't have to stay here.
	Do I?
Una	No.
	You're right.
Ray	I don't have to listen.
	I don't have to say anything.
	So
	but a few minutes

a couple of minutes and then you will have to go
and
because I will be needed back.

He steps on some discarded food in a wrapper,
not noticing it.

Una   Watch.
They haven't finished that.
Someone's just left it there.
You should say something about that.

He picks it up.

Ray   They've been told.
They're constantly being told.

He takes the wrapper to the bin, pushes it in.

A knock at the door.

He walks to the door, opens it a small way to see
who's there.

He steps out, closes it behind him.

Una looks around the room, then sits.

Ray re-enters.

He closes the door but not fully; the same width
as before.

Why don't we go outside?

Una   Where?

Ray   Out of here.
Outside.

Una   No.

Ray   The car park or the

Una   I'm fine here.

Ray	It's
Una	You pushed me in here.
Ray	I didn't push
Una	Out of sight.
Ray	I didn't push you. I brought you in here.
Una	They'll wonder who I am, will they?
Ray	They all saw you. So yes. I'm sure they will. They
Una	You kept me waiting, Peter. I was standing there for
Ray	What do you want? Will you
Una	Can I close the door?
Ray	No.
Una	Can *you* close the door?
Ray	The door stays open.
Una	Why? I
Ray	I don't want it closed.
Una	There's a draught.
Ray	We're going outside in a minute.
Una	I'm here now. You brought me
Ray	I think this is better outside. We can

Una   Close the door.

He doesn't move.

There's a cold draught coming in.
I don't like it.
It's
I'll close it then.

Pause.

She gets up, looks at him, goes to the door.

He takes a step towards her, stops.

She pushes the door shut, suddenly, loudly.

The door's closed.

She looks at some litter near the door.

The people who just
they expect other people to clean up after them.
I asked a man
he dropped an empty can
beer can
and a crisp packet
on the pavement.
Dropped them.
Didn't think about it, just let them fall.
I told him to pick them up.
He laughed.
He thought I was joking.
He was

Ray   Will you

He blinks, rubs at his eyes.

Una   with a woman.
Bitch, she called me.
Defended him.
He laughed all

Ray	How did you find me?
Una	In a It was a photo. In a magazine.
Ray	Where? What
Una	Some
Ray	Magazine?
Una	Trade magazine. Promotional. A glossy magazine thing, a in a waiting room. A doctor's waiting room. You know the thing I'm talking about?
Ray	Yes.
Una	There was a photo on the back of it. You and a with a group of people. A team. They called you a team. You won an award. Some Excellence or performance.
Ray	So What? You saw a photograph? You saw this photo
Una	You have friends?
Ray	And it You

Una	Friends?
Ray	Yes. Of course I have friends, what
Una	New friends or the same old friends?

Pause.

Your eyes are red.
They look like they're stinging.

He laughs briefly to himself, rubbing his eyes again.

Ray	What did you feel?
Una	Don't rub them.
Ray	A photo. So you drove here?
Una	Yes. You want to see it?
Ray	No, I don't want to see it.
Una	But you know the photo I'm
Ray	Yes
Una	Stop rubbing them.
Ray	They hurt.
Una	Because you're rubbing them.
Ray	I rub them *because* they hurt. It's the only way to stop them hurting. You drove here?
Una	Yes.

Ray	How many
	how long did it take you?
	Where
	I don't believe
Una	Is it me?
	Am I making that happen?
	Are you allergic to me?

Pause.

He stares at her.

Are you not going to talk?

| Ray | We're going to walk outside. |

He moves towards her.

On your feet.
Will you get up please?
We're going outside.
We're going to walk through the

Una	I wrote you letters.
Ray	Letters?
Una	They
Ray	I never got any letters.
Una	They were
Ray	When?
Una	never sent.

Pause.

Ray	What did they say?
	When was this?
Una	I wasn't *meant* to send them.
	They told me, the people who helped me.

The
who
afterwards
to write you a letter
letters
telling you what I thought of you.
What I felt.
Wanted to say to you.
To not let it
let you have
win.
Authority.
And it was

Ray   Authority?
        What's

Una   I wrote
        hundreds.
        Pull out your eyes.
        I wrote that I wanted to pull out your eyes, wrote
            poke them out, stamp on them.
        The eyes that'd looked at me.
        The hands.
        To
        All kinds of things.
        I've still got them.

Ray   You kept them?

Una   The best ones.
        I still read them sometimes.
        The fury in them.

        Then I had to write about hope.
        They got me to write about hope.
        What I was able to do.
        What I was free to do now.
        What the future would be

the promising future
the promise the future held
in spite of you
despite you
regardless of you.

You didn't answer.
New friends?
Or did your old friends stand by you?

Ray   What do you think?

Una   I think
I think the fact

Ray   Six seven hours to drive here.
For what?

Una   Because in that photo you're

Ray   To make me suffer?

Una   I wouldn't call that
your eyes
suffering.
Rub them more then.
Harder.

Ray   I didn't need to talk to you.
I could've walked away.
I'm under no

Una   So this man

Ray   What man?

Una   That man who dropped the litter, the
it's not the litter
it wasn't the litter
the dirtying.
It was the man, the person doing that.
Because he hasn't been, been

schooled
educated
civilised enough.
And I thought, and it's
if I walked into his house and dropped litter on
  his carpet.
But the streets, the pavements, they're not my
  house, so
I don't care about the streets.
I just thought you are a beast.
No one has ever cared for you properly and
  you're too stupid
too stupid to even know that or you wouldn't let
  other people see
just what a
see what you are.
This
You do not even know you exist.

I asked to speak to Peter.
And Ray appeared.

Pause.

Ray   This was pointless.
        Absolutely pointless.
        Can you see that?
        Can you not see that?
        Who told you to do this?
        Whoever advised this was

Una   No one.

Ray   The people who
        who helped you.
        Your

Una   I stopped seeing them years ago.
        They're not there for ever.

Ray	The doctor.
	A confrontation
	What do they call it?
	The
	Face-to-face.
	To
	I didn't agree to this.
Una	No.
Ray	To get what?
	You don't have the right to my my my
	humiliation.
	Where I work.
	Where people are.
	My colleagues.
	Work colleagues.
	Walking in, asking for me.
	I've nothing to say to you.
	I
	You're a
	some kind of ghost
	turning up from nowhere to
	Go home.
	Please.
	Leave me alone.
	Go home.
Una	You think I still live in the same city?
Ray	I don't know.
	I don't know where you live.
	How would I know that?
Una	I do.
	I still live there.
	We
Ray	Out of here and

Una	never moved.
Ray	Go back there.
	Go back.
Una	I do feel like a ghost.
	I do.
	I feel like a ghost.
	Everywhere I go.
	I wrote that in my letters too.
	You made me into a ghost.
	People talked about me as if I wasn't there.
	Wouldn't let me speak.
Ray	Go outside.
	Go.
	I'm telling you.
	Listen to me.
	You're
	Walk out into the air.
	Breathe air.
	Get in your car.
	Stop being a ghost.
	You'll
	You will live again.
	Because this this this should
	should never have happened.
	Because are you feeling any better yet?
	Is this doing you *good*?
Una	Yes.
Ray	Then that's
	That is
	I can't say anything to you.
	You
	You're beyond
	How?
	How the hell is it good?

Tell me
except
except but you don't know what you want.
You don't know why you're here.
Tell whoever it was sent you

Una   Nobody.
        I told you.

Ray   Then I don't care.

        He makes to go.

Una   Where are you going?

Ray   No.

Una   Don't go.

Ray   I don't care.
        It's not my responsibility.

Una   I'll follow you.

Ray   Do what you want.
        This is
        This is hell.

        Stay away from me.
        You need help.

        He's at the door.

        He goes out.

Una   Ray.
        Don't leave me in here.

        He re-enters, closes the door.

        Pause.

Ray   I have things I have to do.
        I have to check things.

	And
	After.
	When I leave.
	Tonight.
	I have to be places.
	People are relying on me.
Una	What?
	What're you doing?
Ray	The thing is
	The
	I don't even know if it *is* you.
	If you're
	her.
Una	I am.
	Of course I am.
Ray	I didn't recognise you.
Una	Yes you did.
Ray	I didn't.
	I *don't*.
	You.
	No.
Una	Your face went white.
Ray	Not
Una	Drained white.
Ray	Not not when I saw you.
	I didn't know who you were.
	There's a woman here to see you.
	That's all I was told.
Una	When I said
Ray	Yes

yes but I know the name.
I remember the name.
Jesus the name's
But you could be a, a friend of hers.
Your hair's a different colour.
A journalist.
A

Una   I'm not.

Ray   Reporter, I don't know.
      I don't know what any of this is meant to be.

Una   How many other twelve-year-old girls have you
      had sex with?

      Pause.

Ray   None.

Una   Do you want to see the birthmark?
      You kissed it.
      Or what you said to me on the beach.
      Pointing across the sea to
      to Holland.
      Or on the bed in that room in

      None?
      We change, twelve-year-olds.
      We grow up to be older.
      So think.

Ray   None.

Una   Just me.
      In that room.

      I thought it'd be harder to look at you.
      To talk.
      I nearly turned back.
      But it's not.
      It's easy.

And I would've recognised you anywhere.
With my back to you.
I saw your eyes before I even said my name.
I saw you.

You have someone?
You live with someone?
You don't want to tell me.
I know you're with a woman.
The way I was looked at outside.
The way *you* were looked at when you walked
    towards me.
A good woman?
Does she

Ray   I'm not talking about her with

Una   Is she expecting you home?

      Pause.

Ray   D'you want me to say something?
      Is there anything you want me to say now?

Una   Does she know about me?

Ray   I will not say anything about my life.
      Who is in my life.
      If that's what you wanted to find out and I don't
          know why you
      you would want that
      but you're getting nothing.
      Do you understand?
      Do you understand?

      Pause.

Una   My dad died.

      You didn't know?
      It didn't reach you?

He shakes his head.

Six years ago.
Maybe you weren't here.
Maybe you were somewhere else.

Ray   I was here.
How?

Una   He fell down.
He tripped.
Steps.
And
Deteriorated.
He never got over it.
He
You were a guest in our home.
I was his baby.
He invited you as a guest into his home.
He tried to find you.

Ray   He knew where I was the first four years.

Una   He wanted to kill you.
Not a second thought.
He said it all the time.
It was
He would've killed you.

Ray is startled, unnerved by her loudness and tone.

Near tears, Una searches through her bag.

Ray watches her, unsettled.

Ray   What's in there?

What's in your bag?
What's in it?

Una   I need a

Ray	Give me it
Una	No.
	Why?
Ray	What're you doing?
	Are you
Una	What?
Ray	Don't.

He grabs the bag from her.

Una	You're
Ray	Do you want to kill me?

Pause.

He goes through the bag.

He takes out a packet of tissues.

Una	I was going to Kleenex you to death.

She holds out her hand.

He gives her the packet.

He takes out a bottle of water.

And that's acid, not water.

He takes out the torn page from the trade magazine.

The photo of him.

A knock on the door.

A voice from behind the door.

Voice	Peter.

Pause.

They look at each other.

Ray goes to the door.

He opens the door slightly, looks out through the gap.

Ray   (*to person outside*) It's fine.

He closes the door.

He still holds the photo.

Una   When I saw it I
the photo.
It's not clear.
But I knew it was you.
I tore it out, took it home, kept
kept looking at it.
The name below.
Peter.
Peter?
I couldn't
I'm so slow sometimes.
You changed your name.

Ray   Yes.

Una   Is that difficult?

Ray   No.
No, it was very easy.

Una   But I mean, decide.
Decide on a new one.
Choose a new name.
Is it hard?
Do you do you go through
how many before you decide?
Do you make a list?

Ray   I chose a name at random.

Una	How?
Ray	I opened the phone book.
Una	Pin the tail on the donkey.
Ray	Kind of.
Una	What's your full name? Peter what? Peter I can ask outside.
Ray	Trevelyan.
Una	Peter Trevelyan.
Ray	Yes.

Pause. She gives a quick smile, smothers it.

Una	Where the hell did that come from? Peter *Trevelyan?*
Ray	Under T. It was necessary. It
Una	But Jesus. *Trevelyan.* Did you God, no That's To To the manor born. The silver spoon. It's from a phone book at *random?* Were you delirious? Did delusions of of grandeur?

Because
Jesus.
The rich sleep
sleep with young girls too.
Under-age girls.
Ruin their lives too.
In fact the rich must have as much sex with
     young girls as the poor.
They must be neck and neck.
But if it does the job.
If it
Does it?
Command respect?
And help you
Help you

Ray   Okay.

Una   forget.

Ray   Enough.

Una   They don't know.
      Any of them, outside.
      Do they?
      And your
      The partner?
      She
      The the lady of the manor.
      No one

Ray   She knows.

Una   She knows?

Ray   Yes.

Una   How does she know?

Ray   I told her.

Una	Everything?
Ray	The facts.
Una	My age?
Ray	Yes.
Una	Your sentence?
Ray	Yes.
Una	When? At the start of the
Ray	Yes. We've been together seven years.
Una	What did you tell her? What? Tell me what you told her?
Ray	That when I was forty I had I had an illegal relationship. I had sex with a minor.
Una	And she was fine with that?
Ray	No. Of course not. But I I told her what my life was like then. I wasn't in a good way. I had problems and I didn't I couldn't handle them. I gave in. I broke apart.
Una	Did you?
Ray	I made the biggest most most stupid mistake of my life.

Una	You told her it was a
Ray	A what?
Una	A three-month stupid mistake you made. That you ran away with me. That too?
Ray	And that I pulled myself up. I I got back on track. I You laugh. You don't believe it. That's fine. It's fine with me. I don't need you to.
Una	She believed you. You managed to make her believe
Ray	Because she loves me.
Una	What's wrong with her? Must be something wrong with her.
Ray	Don't Do not say that. Don't talk about her. She she has helped me.
Una	Do you have any children with her?
Ray	No.
Una	Do you want children?
Ray	That's not funny.
Una	D'you see me laughing? No, I think it is.

She laughs briefly.

He turns away.

In that photo there's nothing.
Nothing in your face.
Smiling.
You've forgotten.
You've

Ray   Yes.
Yes I have.

Una   Ten years later
Eight
eight years
now
you'd be on the register.
Your name would be there.
Ray would be there.
You'd be
You wouldn't be able to forget.
You couldn't
Peter
You'd
No one would let you.
It wouldn't just be me.
People would be outside your
surrounding your house.

Ray   I'm living my life.
A new life that I fought for because I lost

Una   Did you ever think about me?

Ray   I have every right.
I can push it as far away as I

Una   What was happening to me?

Ray   You think I should relive it every day?
      This is my life.
      You can't

Una   When that judge

Ray   You can't come in and

Una   Six years.
      And when my parents told me.

Ray   I am entitled to something.
      To live.

Una   *I* did the sentence.
      I did your sentence.
      For fifteen years.
      I lost everything.
      I lost more than you ever did.
      I lost
      because I never had
      had time to to to *begin*.
      We never moved.
      That house in that street.
      I was talked about, pointed at, stared at.
      I lost all my friends.
      I
      I *kept* my name.
      I had to keep my name.
      I
      Yes.
      I re-live it every day.

Ray   If you want me to
      whatever it is you want me to
      I've taken you seriously.
      But if you tell me
      You can't think about it every day.

Una   I don't have to think.
      It's *there*.

Ray	Is that wise?
	No.
	To
	To let yourself?
	To
	Does no one tell you it's
	D'you not have friends
	people who
Una	Of course I have friends.
Ray	Who know that you do this?
Una	Yes.
Ray	And they listen?
	They still
Una	Yes.
Ray	What kind of friends are they?
	What kind of
Una	Don't talk about
Ray	They *allow* this?
	They actually
	They're waiting to hear from you are they?
	How this went?
	How
	Are they outside?
	Did they drive you here?
	Are they
Una	There's no one with me.
	How many times do I have to tell you?
Ray	Do you
	a partner?
	A
Una	That's nothing to do with this.

29

Ray   Does anyone care about you at all?

        Pause.

        I've done the same.
        I've brought you in here
        Let let you talk.
        And I was
        and listened and

Una   What about the photos?

Ray   What do you do?
        Do you work?
        Are you able to work?
        Have you taken time off to

Una   The photos.

Ray   What photos?

Una   The photos you took of me.
        In your flat.
        Where are they?
        They never found them.

Ray   I

Una   The police never found them.

Ray   They

Una   I've seen websites.
        Hundreds on websites.
        Hundreds of nine, ten, eleven, twelve years old.
        Younger.
        Photographed in
        on beds
        in bedrooms and
        Am I one?
        Because these
        some of

the photos go back to the seventies
they
you can tell by the room
and people, men *scan* them and put them, they
those kids'll be adults now and not know they're

Ray   I burnt them.

Una   Did you?

Ray   Yes.
Of course I did.
Of course.
No one ever saw them.
I burnt them before we
Before we left.
And they weren't
You were wearing your clothes, jeans
They

Una   Sitting on your sofa.
Lying down.
They've the same photos on

Ray   Those sites.
That
Those people.
Those sick bastards.
I was never one of them.
I was never that.
You
you've been told I was, I am, I
They called me that.
They

Una makes to go.

What're you doing?

Una   I want to leave here.

Ray	No. I was not one of them. Never. They
Una	Let me out.
Ray	Wait.
Una	Let me
Ray	I need a minute. Sit down.
Una	No.
Ray	Sit down.
Una	Don't come near me.
Ray	Not like this. Don't
Una	I want to get out of here. Get away from the door.
Ray	Listen to me.
Una	Move over there.
Ray	Listen. I spent three years in hell. More.
Una	Yes.
Ray	What they called me. Spat on, kicked. Shit, human shit thrown in my face. You know I wasn't one of them.
Una	How
Ray	You know.

Una	I don't know you.
	I don't know anything about you except that
	you abused me.
	Didn't you?
	Didn't you?
Ray	Yes.
	But
Una	There's no but.
Ray	Let me
Una	There is no but.
Ray	Yes.
	I did.
	But
Una	Jesus.
Ray	I didn't
	I didn't
Una	Didn't what?
Ray	They said in court I, I
	made it sound
	made it look
	that I'd *selected* you.
	I'd chosen
	That day.
	That day of the barbecue.
	At
	When we talked for the first time.
	I didn't come to
	You know.

On his belt, his mobile phone rings.

When I spoke to you for the first time.
I
Wait.

He looks at the phone's screen.

He turns it off.

Pause.

Una Was that her?

Ray Yes.

Can I have some water?

He takes the bottle of water, drinks from it.

I don't know why he invited me, your father.
I said hello to him on the street when I saw him.
I helped him with his car once.
But
I was surprised when he asked me.
I wasn't going to come.
I didn't know anyone there.
Or neighbours who
But I

My windows were open and I could smell the
    barbecue.
Five doors away.
The smoke.

It wasn't to
because of you
to
I'd seen you in the street.
Around.
But not
Not

Una	You were looking at me. At the barbecue.
Ray	No.
Una	I saw you
Ray	I wasn't.
Una	I felt you.
Ray	I *looked* at you. I wasn't *looking*.
Una	You said why aren't you happy? You should be happy. The first thing you said.
Ray	Yes. You were sitting on your own. Not talking to anyone. You weren't very happy. *That's* what I was watching. You People tried to talk to you and you you gave them nothing. You'd You'd fallen out with your best friend. Hadn't you?
Una	I used to think After. If we hadn't fallen out. If she'd been there. It could've been her.
Ray	How many people were there? How many guests? Fifteen, twenty. In your garden. Your parents' small garden and

You know when you are
A person knows.
I read this
when they're aroused by children
by under-age
people.

Una   You read it?

Ray   Yes.

Una   There's a handbook?

Ray   There's

Una   A checklist?

Ray   Because when you're aroused by children
when

Una   I read some of those books too.

Ray   So have I.
So did I.
As many as I could find
To to
Yes, a checklist.
It was, yes.
To find out
to
to learn the facts.

Una   What facts?

Ray   The facts.
The patterns.
The the cycle.

Una   The cycle?

Ray   Of of

Una   Abuse.

Ray	Yes.
Una	Can't you say it?
Ray	Abuse.
	Abusing.
	There's figures
Una	Were you abused as a child?
Ray	No.
Una	You're sure?
Ray	Yes.
	For God's sake.
	Don't
	I feel sick.
	I think I'd remember that.
	The lawyer asked me if I *had* been.
	It was better for me if I had been.
	Better better for everyone if I had been.
	I read those books.
	I thought about my life.
	To be sure I wasn't one of them, one of
	Because four years being told
	asked to ask myself
	interrogate myself.
	Being given no
	Because when you are
	when kids
	when they they do it for
	for a person
	but they don't want to to admit
	they're shocked
	horrified that they
	they feel like this.
	They stay away.

They're a threat and they know it.
They distance themselves.
They
Because they love them but
they love them too much to
to want to show that love because that love is
They want to protect them.
They stay away from wherever children will be.

But if you're aroused.
Do desire.
And want to want to
feed that desire
they find ways
they
they're always looking for ways to be near them.
To lure them.
These people are
very very careful
are very very deceptive.
The greater the deception
the greater the risk
the more they enjoy it.

Una   Did you memorise these books?

Ray   It was a hot day.
        The day of the barbecue.
        I
        and I had a pair of shorts on.
        My *only* pair of shorts.
        I only ever own one pair at a time.
        I wear one pair until they're old and then buy
            new ones.
        Because I don't

Una   What

Ray   wear shorts.

Una	Are you
Ray	I never wear shorts unless it's very hot.
Una	*Shorts?*
Ray	And they were tight shorts. It was the style then. The Don't smile. Don't I'm trying to tell you. Don't They laughed in court. They laughed at that in court. I remember these shorts.
Una	Do you hear yourself? Your tight shorts? Do you know how
Ray	If I had an erection
	If I had an erection. Aroused. I was standing beside you. I would've I would've walked away from you or sat down or because when I had an erection in those shorts it was You couldn't miss it. It was obvious. Any person looking could plainly see any guest would've seen. They would've And it's not I know it's not the only indication

but but it is for me.
When I am
when I
turned on I go hard.
I go hard immediately.
But I stayed there.
I stayed there and talked to you.
You were someone's
a neighbour's daughter who
who was annoyed at the world that day.
Not not a
target.
I never

I had a
I was seeing a woman.
And I know they
those people can have relationships
and still do what they do.
But most of them not
don't.
They're loners.
Incapable of having a

Pause.

Una   My parents thought you were

Ray   What?

Una   Shy.
A bit dull.
And a loner.
Why you hadn't brought your girlfriend.
My dad said you could bring her.

Ray   She wasn't my girlfriend.
She was

Una   You saw a lot of her.

Ray   I only saw her for a few months.
       I can't even remember her name.
       She was dull.

Una   She attacked me once.
       A couple of years later.
       I was with my mother walking on the street.
       She came up to me and slapped me on the face.

       Pause.

Ray   She said you used to glare at her.
       That you were, were after me.
       You'd hang around on the street beside my car.

Una   I made up with my friend.
       I told her about you.
       About talking to you.
       You you looking at me.
       Flirting.

Ray   That was you, not me.
       You
       The notes.
       You wrote notes.
       You put them under the windscreen wipers of
          my car.
       Your girlfriend's ugly.
       She has a glass eye.
       Always one sentence.
       She laughs like a donkey.

Una   That's not

Ray   And others.
       Remember the barbecue.
       That was one.
       I had to tell you to stop it.
       Outside the newsagents.
       And you said what was I talking about.
       You pretended not to know.

41

Una	I did stop.
	I stopped writing them.
	I'd have done anything you said.
	I wanted you to be my boyfriend.
	I wanted to sit beside you in your car and be driven into town.
	And for people to see me.
	See *us*.
	I took a Polaroid of you and
	with my friend
	we kissed it
	we
	put it on my pillow and slept beside it.
	And I
	any excuse.
	Brought you biscuits and some cake that my mother made.
	Asked you to sponsor me for a sponsored walk.
	I
	oh I was shameless.
	You didn't stop that.
	All you had to do was tell my parents.
	A stupid girl who had a stupid crush.
	But you didn't.
	You let it start.
Ray	You weren't stupid.
Una	Yes I was.
Ray	You weren't.
Una	If I wasn't stupid I'd have known what was happening.
	But I didn't.
	I was too young.
	Too too in
	love.

Too stupid not to have been older
not to have have
the awareness
the experience.
But that's what you wanted.
I didn't ask difficult questions.
I didn't have any questions *to* ask.
I wanted anything you wanted.

Ray   No.

Una   Yes.
I said yes and I kept saying yes.
Eager to please.
Desperate to please.

Ray   You don't remember yourself.
What you were like.

Una   What was I like?

Ray   Strong.

Una   Strong?
What does that mean?

Ray   Headstrong.

Una   Don't.

Ray   Determined.

Una   Don't.

Ray   When we started to talk properly.
Alone.
When you told me about yourself.
I discovered
You surprised me.
You made me laugh.

Una   Laugh?

Did I
what?
Pull faces?

Ray   I

Una   *Tickle* you?

Ray   You were older than her.
That woman I was seeing.

Una   *Older?*

Ray   With that stupid laugh.
Yes.

Una   How, older?
You're not making any

Ray   You knew about love.
You knew more about love than she did.
Than *I* did.
You knew what you wanted.
So so impatient.
You couldn't wait to start menstruating.
You told me that.
You were sick of being treated like a child.
The last thing you wanted was to be told you
    were a child.

Una   Jesus.

Ray   You

Una   That's what children *say.*

Ray   You weren't like other children.

Una   I was a girl.
A virgin.
An untouched body.
A

Having it to yourself.
Being the first.
Teaching me.
Showing me.

Ray   No.

Una   Coming inside me.
What could I have possibly given you
given you that *wasn't* my twelve-year-old body?
What else could you have wanted?
There was nothing else.

Ray   There was.
For me there was.

She walks away from him.

In prison.
The sessions.
Group sessions.
The raking over of of everything.
What went wrong.
What was missing.
My my status
Lack of status.
The anger I had.
Blaming others.
The urge to destroy.
Because that's what they told me I'd done.
Destroyed.
Destroyed you.
Your family.
My parents.
My life.
And what drove me wasn't the love I felt.
Something
something rotten.
Something deeper.

You were on my mind all the time.
I couldn't get you out.
And I gave in.
I gave in to it.
And it
everything
every day was about how I could see you, talk
    to you.
I left work early.
I, I'd work on my car on the street.
It didn't need work.
I took things apart, put them back together.
Just to
The engine was perfect.
But I'd
Because you'd be there and we could talk and
    it was fine.
It was in the open and no one thought anything.
Your parents.
The kids that played there.
But it, it wasn't enough, it
I had to be alone with you.

You remember the
the codes
the the signals we had to to meet.
To just speak.
Talk.
To be alone together.
You remember?
I'd phone your parents' house.
One ring.

Una   It meant that she wasn't with you.
        You were on your own.

Ray   And park my car facing right.

46

Una   I forgot that.
      And the next day you'd be there to meet me.
      In the park.
      The public park.

Ray   It was the only place we could meet.

Una   The first time.
      In the park.

      I'd be so excited.
      Knowing you'd be there.
      And I ran.
      Because you were mine.
      You were sitting on a bench reading a newspaper.
      And the first thing you said to me
      You told me not to sit down beside you.
      I had to walk past you.
      And I knew why.

Ray   It was ridiculous.
      Stupid place to meet.
      I hadn't thought about it.
      I, I *didn't* think.
      I didn't know what was happening to me.
      And you

Una   I walked into the bushes.

Ray   You disappeared.
      And started calling out my name.
      Ray.
      Come here, Ray.
      I sat there and
      a man
      there was a man walking along the path.
      You called out again and he looked at me and
          laughed.
      He hadn't seen you.

He didn't *know*.
Only heard your voice.
Ray, come on.
I'm waiting.
And I
I'd been seen but I could still explain it.
Up to that moment I would still be believed.
I could walk away and stop everything.

Una   But you didn't.

Ray   No.
I couldn't.
Whatever was happening
whatever I was thinking
thought about
was in me
made me believe I loved you.
Made me walk across the grass, the
get on my knees and crawl under the branches.
and hold your hand and
and kiss you.

Una   And lay down next to each other.
And open my shirt and touch my
my breasts.
And and unzip yourself.
And take out your prick.

Ray   Not the first time.

Una   I'm sorry.
You you *gentleman*.
Not the first time.
The second, the third time.
Both of us lying on a blanket you brought.
A blanket.
I thought it was for me but it was

Ray	It was.
Una	so that twigs and and earth and wouldn't stick to my clothes. So no one would suspect.
Ray	I didn't want us to get caught.
	I've never loved Never desired anyone that age again. Ever.
Una	Just me.
Ray	Yes. Just you. You were the only one.

Pause.

It never came up in the trial.
The park, the bushes.
The blanket.
I always wondered why.

Una	I never told them.
Ray	Why?
Una	I was I don't know. You didn't either.
Ray	No. They'd have given me ten years.

Pause.

Una	I was only in court for a day. Behind that screen. I never knew what was said. No one told me anything.

I was at a relative's house.
Not allowed to leave.
No television, no newspapers.
No one told me about the trial.
Even now my mother won't
What was the name of the town?
Where we
we went.
There was a beach.
We drove there to get the ferry.
It was dark.
Winter.
The shops were shuttered.
What was its name?

Ray   Why?

Una   I want to know.
I couldn't find it anywhere.
What was its name?
We walked along the beach.
It was cold.
We held hands.
We could do that because it was dark.
You pointed out to sea.
Across the sea to where we were going.
Can you see it?
There it is.
You got a room at a guest house.
I had to stand behind you as you paid the woman.
Keep my head down and run up the stairs.
Did you know her?
That woman.

Ray   No.

Una   I always thought you did.
I don't know why.

Ray	No.
	How would I?
	No.
	What
Una	There were twin beds
Ray	Okay.
Una	Why not?
Ray	I've told you why.
	It's
	I don't want to hear it.
Una	I do.
Ray	We both know what happened.
Una	I don't.
	I don't know everything.
	You don't.
	You don't know anything.
	I want you to know.
	What I did for you.
Ray	What you did for me?
Una	What was the name of the town?
Ray	Tynemouth.
	Pause.
Una	Twin beds.
	A TV.
	Nothing else.
	The window looking out at the sea.
	We undressed.
	We had sex on one of the beds.
	I don't know how long for.
	I saw how much pleasure it gave you.

I liked I could do that.
We did it twice, fucked twice.
You turned me round for the second time.
You made so much noise.
We lay in each other's arms afterwards.
I cried a bit.
My parents would be looking for me.
They'd be phoning my friend
maybe at the school asking where I was
why I wasn't home
had anyone seen me?

Pause.

You said you wanted cigarettes.
You were going to look for a shop, a pub.
I wanted to go with you but you said no I was to
    wait there, wait for you.
You'd be five minutes.
And you touched me you
kissed me between my legs
your tongue
both of my breasts.
You'd be back in no time.

I lay on the bed.
I listened to your footsteps going downstairs.
I wrapped the sheet around me and went over to
    the window.
I wanted chocolate
I tried to open it.
Whatever I ate then.
Sweets.
Shout to you.
Chocolate.
But the window wouldn't open.
I saw you down below, opening the front gate.
I knocked on the window but you

you were already walking along the street, the
   middle of the street.
You didn't hear me.

I fell asleep and when I woke up I didn't know
   the time.
I was sore between my legs but I felt wonderful.
You hadn't come back yet but I was so happy.
My man would be back soon and he would have
   chocolate for me.
I didn't need to tell him what I wanted.
You knew and you'd bring it to me.
But you still didn't come.

The room was cold.
I got dressed, looked out the window.
Your car was still there across the road.
I could hear talking downstairs, not clearly.
But voices.
I walked down the stairs.
The front door was closed.
The only sound was a TV coming from a room.
The voices were from the TV.
The door was open a bit.
I knocked on the door.
Nothing happened.
No one was there.
I opened the front door and went out.
There was a shout as I was closing the door.
The woman.
I opened
saw her
what are you or
saw her walking towards me
and I, I shut the door and
ran to the gate and out into the street and ran.

I walked into the centre of town.

It was late.
Ten on the church clock.
The ferry left at midnight.
There wasn't long.
You were nowhere.
A shop was open, lights.
I asked inside if a man had bought some cigarettes.
He told me to get out.
He thought *I* was buying cigarettes.
I tried to describe you but he didn't listen.

Then a pub.
The first pub.
You'd be inside having a drink and a smoke.
But I couldn't go in
I had to
all my courage
wait till two men walked in
follow behind them
and look for you
walking around the pub.
Men making jokes, laughing.
What was I wanting?
You lost, hinny?

I said my dad.
The man behind the bar asked me
We said I'd
in trouble
you were my dad.
Told him what you wearing, what you looked like.
He'd seen you.
You'd been in.
The accent.
Smoked a cigarette, had a drink, then left.
He was concerned, the man.
He asked me my name and I told him.

He wanted to walk with me, help me look.
I said no, no, no, I'm fine, I'm fine.
I kept walking.
Along the main street.
A few people passed me.
I wanted to ask them if they'd seen you but
    I didn't know what to say.
I went into another pub, another.
Everyone's face turning to look at me, shouting,
    laughing.

I walked on and on.
The next pub, the next.
People staring, laughing, telling me to get out.
I walked past houses
getting further from the sea.
I walked ten paces, ran ten.
You'd be at the next corner, the next.
Any moment.
And every car was you.
The houses stopped.
I was at the end of the town.
The road carried on.
I looked out into the dark countryside.
I'd gone too far.
I'd walked too far.
I was at the end.
You
I'd missed you.
You were back at the guest house.
Looking for me, wondering where I was.
I'd
I ran.
I ran back.
I thought I was lost and then I wasn't.
I could see the clock above the roofs.
I walked towards it.

It was half-eleven.
We could still make the ferry.
I ran and ran.
I could see the guest house.
But your car had gone.
I checked
ran up and down looking into all the cars but
and my bag was inside your car
with all my clothes
with everything.
And you were gone.
The clothes I'd brought.
But
and
my passport in my pocket and that
I
The room
but it was dark, the window.
I didn't know what to do.
Waited.
I sat on a bench.
I was freezing, hungry.
I wanted to know why you'd gone.
What I had done.
I was crying.
You'd left me.
You'd
Or something terrible had happened.
You'd been killed or drowned or
I couldn't do anything, couldn't go anywhere.
We wouldn't be on the ferry.
We wouldn't be leaving.
I didn't know what to do.
Something had happened.
You wouldn't have left me.
You wouldn't have done that.

I heard midnight.
You weren't coming.
I was alone.
A woman talked to me.
They saw me and crossed the road.
A man and a woman walking their dog.
They asked what I was doing there.
Where did I live?
Who was looking after me?
I went back to their house.
They gave me blankets and phoned my parents.
I lay on their sofa and listened to her talk to my
    mother.
The police were there with her.
I felt sick.
I wanted to die.
I was never going to see you again.
I'd have to face all of them
everyone
all of them
alone.

I protected you.
Defended you.
Stayed
stayed true.
I told the police you hadn't touched me.
You'd done nothing.
I was a
I was a runaway.
I wanted to escape my parents, my house,
    my school.
You'd given me a lift in your car.
You helped me escape.
I'd asked you, begged you.
You'd driven me there and left.

You won't know any of this.

They wanted to do tests.
Take samples out of me.
Doctors, police.
I refused.
No one was going to touch me.
I shouted, screamed
You'd done nothing.
You'd
I wanted you to
I wanted you back.
I
They drugged me.
Held me down and and injected me.
Opened my legs and took
took out your come.
Evidence.
They asked me what you'd done to me.
Then told me what you'd done to me when
    I wouldn't.
You were only after one thing.
That's why you'd disappeared.
You'd got what you wanted.
My my mother screaming at me.
She
The police, the
a woman psychiatrist who spoke
always spoke so quietly.
Adults lie.
They want things from people and they lie to get
    them and, and don't
they don't even know they're lying.
They do not know themselves.
I couldn't hear her sometimes.
Had to ask
repeat

repeat what she'd said.
Did I know what I'd done?
Did I know that I'd hurt people?
People who loved me.
Did did I want to hurt them?
And
For days.
What had you said?
What did you promise me?
What words
What words did you use?

And in the courtroom I sat behind that screen
    and I spoke.
I cried.
You heard me.
I cried more than I spoke.
And then I
I said too much, I
The lawyers were furious with me.
It wasn't what they wanted.
I couldn't help it.
It was you.
You were there and I couldn't see you so I had
    to shout.
I had to let you know.
You left me alone.
Bleeding.
You left me.
You left me in love.

When they came home at the end
into the house.
My parents.
Not home.
The relatives' house.
I was in the bedroom, waiting.

They were silent.
They didn't move.
I sat and waited.
They didn't come through to me.
I thought maybe you'd got off.
You'd been let go.
You'd be coming back to live beside us.
Until my dad
later
told me six years.
And in the night I woke up and my mother was
    there.
Leaning over me.
Shouting that *they'd* been tried.
She'd been on the stand.
And my dad had to take her out of the room.
Pull her out of the room.
And
The judge.
What he said about me.
You'll remember.
I had
suspicious
suspiciously adult yearnings.
When my mother told me that I didn't know
    what she meant.

And we never moved house.
They
To, to shame me.
To punish me.
So I'd be pointed at.
And slapped in the street.
Or the psychiatrist told them it was better to stay.
For for continuity or

I hate the life I've had.

You wouldn't know that.
I wanted you to know that.
I knew you'd forget about me.

Ray   I wrote you a letter.
After a year in there.
I sent one.
They let me send one.
They had to read them first.
Did you get it?

Una   No.
I didn't get any letters.

Ray   They'd have told your parents.

Una   What did it say?

Ray   To forgive me.
Explaining.
Apologising.
What I'd learnt about myself.

Pause.

There was another letter
One they wouldn't let me send.
I thought it would be good for you to read it.

I came back.
I was coming back for you.

Pause.

I bought

Una   Coming back?

Ray   Yes.
I did buy cigarettes.
I
Listen.

Una	Is this what you tell yourself?
Ray	It's what happened. I bought the cigarettes but I went
Una	Is this what you use? To to For this? To smile in a photo.
Ray	No. Listen. There was a pub. I Listen. I had a drink. I needed time. I needed to think, to plan. The ferry, the passports. How to explain. What to say. And I needed a drink. I needed courage. It was going to happen. I walked around for a while. The streets. Behind, around. I knew you were waiting for me. But I had to Until I was back there, at the guest house. Looking up at the window. The light in the window. The woman was there. Stripping the sheets. She said you'd gone. You'd ran off. What was going on? I left her.

I walked out.
You weren't at the car where I thought you'd be.
Or the beach.
I shouted for you.
I thought you were hiding.
I drove into the town looking for you.
I couldn't find you.
I didn't know where you'd go.
Why you'd gone.
I started to panic.
I thought the police would appear any minute,
    surround my car.
I parked.
I went back into the pub.
The same pub and ordered another drink.
He didn't move, the man there, the same man
    who'd served me.
He was staring at me.
He asked me about my daughter.
Had, had I found her?
And I
I looked at him and said yes, yes I had, she was
    fine.
There was another man beside me.
Asking if I *had* a daughter and what was her name.
I
and I
Another man was getting up from his seat.
The first one leaned over the bar, tried to grab me.
I pulled away, swore at them.
They
Told them
Three, four of them after me.
I ran out.
They chased me.
Two kept chasing me.

I hid
ran somewhere, a
I lost them.
I hid there for, I don't know, an hour.
I heard the clock strike midnight.
I got back to the car and, and drove away and
I didn't know if you'd gone to the police or
if I was leaving you
but I couldn't stay.
I drove to Newcastle.
To where the ferry left from.
If maybe you'd gone somehow, gone there.
Waiting for me there.
I waited till dawn.
Then I knew it was over.

I kept driving.
I didn't know where to go.
I drove west.
I heard the news on the radio.
Safe and well.
Found in Tynemouth by a couple walking their
    dog.
The police were hunting me.
Hunting my car.
They gave out the licence-plate number.
I drove to the coast.
Kept to small roads.
I left the car behind.
Walked.
The Solway Firth.
Found a phonebox, phoned the police.
Waited there till they came.
I'd never have left you there.

Pause.

Una   But there's no difference.

Leaving or coming back.
There's

Ray   There is.
For me there is.

Una   Better for you.
Easier for you.

Ray   It's not easier.
It's
The lawyer

Una   Why say it?
Why say it now?

Ray   The lawyer said it sounded better if I had left
        you there
because it showed I knew the seriousness
the awfulness of what I had done.
That I ran from you.
Never to to return.
Because of what it would sound like to a jury
be *made* to sound like
That I was going back for
for *more*.
Because what else would I go back to you for?

When I couldn't find you that night.
I thought something must've happened to you.
I knew you wouldn't leave me.
Someone had taken you.
Someone was
harming you.
Even thought maybe
maybe I should go to the police.

When they found me I was on the floor of the
        phone box.
Hugging my knees.

Crying my eyes out.
Because I'd lost you.
I, I hadn't protected you.

It does make me feel better.
That I was coming back.
It does.
Whoever I was then.
It makes me feel better.

Una   Why didn't you send the letter?

Ray   I told you.
        They wouldn't let me.

Una   There must have been some way.

Ray   No.

        Pause.

        She stares at him.

        The lights shut off suddenly, in the room and in the windows.

Una   What's happened?
        What's happened.

Ray   I don't

        Una backs against the wall.

Una   What's going on?

Ray   I have to go and see.

Una   Is something wrong?

Ray   No.
        Wait here.

Una   Where are you going?

Ray	I have to find out what's Stay here. Okay?
Una	Yes.
Ray	I'll be one minute. It's probably a power failure or but Wait here.

He opens the door, goes out.

Una waits, very still.

Outside, distant sound of doors closing.

A minute passes.

Una	Ray. Ray.

She walks to the door, looks out into the darkness, afraid.

She turns back.

The light comes back on in the room but not the windows.

Ray re-enters.

Ray	They're unbelievable.
Una	Who?
Ray	Them. All of them. They left.
Una	All of them?
Ray	Yes. To go home.

Una	Are the doors locked?
	Are we
Ray	No.
	No.
	I have keys.
	I lock up.
Una	Why didn't they tell you?
Ray	I don't know.
	They
	They're stupid bastards.
	What's wrong?
	One of them must've just
	not thinking.
	They're
Una	You lock up?
Ray	I have keys.
	I'm usually the last
Una	You'll lock up tonight?
Ray	Yes.
	Why?
Una	Are you the
Ray	What?
Una	The night watchman?
	The, the
	security?
Ray	No.
Una	The caretaker, the janitor?
	Are you
Ray	No.

Una	They must think you are to
Ray	I'm not.
Una	To leave you here.
Ray	I am not
Una	You haven't finished clearing up. You'd
Ray	In a
Una	better start.
Ray	In a shirt?
Una	Look at all this.
Ray	And trousers like these. And these
Una	You've got
Ray	shoes?
Una	some kind of fixation.
Ray	It didn't say my *caretaking* team, the photo. What d'you mean, fixation? What?
Una	Trousers, shorts.
Ray	What're you talking about? I'm I have a position here.
	Pause.
Una	I don't know who I'm looking at.
Ray	I worked to get this. I worked to get here.
Una	Do *you* know?

Ray	Everything was finished for me.
	Closed to me.
Una	Does *anyone*?
Ray	I slaved.
	To *not* be a janitor.
	A caretaker.
	A drunk.
	A
	a waste.
	To rescue something from the
Una	You haven't changed.
	You still just talk
	talk to get, to
	Lie and don't even know you're
Ray	Shut up.
Una	I don't know what to believe, Ray.
	There's so much to choose from.
	Do you live in here?
Ray	What?
Una	Maybe all
Ray	What're you talking about?
Una	the food is yours.
	This is yours.
	You live here and you
	you never leave.
	You never
	You don't have anyone.
Ray	I have someone.
Una	You live here and eat here and
Ray	I found someone.
	I

Una	Does she know Does she know you were coming back to me? Did you tell her that?
	You haven't told her. Have you? You haven't told her anything.
Ray	I wanted to. I wanted to but I wouldn't And we have a life. I've done better than anything anything I could
Una	You
Ray	could imagine. From that phone-box. From that that Crying on his knees. I've My parents. Family. When I was inside. The friends. Nothing for me. Refused to do anything. My flat was repossessed. I had debts. I had nothing. But I found her. And I am the luckiest
Una	Jesus.
Ray	most most grateful man.
Una	Can I meet her?
Ray	Don't be stupid.

Una	But I'm not stupid, Ray.
	You said I wasn't stupid.
	I want to meet her.
	This wonderful woman.
	Who'd never forgive you if she knew.
	Who'd
	Describe her.
	What does she look like?
Ray	Why?
Una	C'mon.
	What does she look like?
Ray	No.
Una	Is she pretty?
	Attractive?

Ray turns away from her.

Una pursues him, getting closer to him.

	Blonde, brunette?
	Tall or short?
	Smart or stupid?
	Ignorant.
	You coward.
	To live like this.
Ray	Why don't you shut your mouth?
Una	I would hate to be her.
	How old is she?
	What's the age difference?
	How much
Ray	One year.
	She's one year older than me.
Una	So she's old like you.
	She's sixty.

Ray	She's not sixty.
Una	You're almost sixty.

Ray turns away from her.

Is she still sexy?
Does she still turn you on?

Ray	Yes.
Una	What does she do to you?
Ray	Jesus.
Una	What d'you like? All that sagging skin. What's she do best?
Ray	You're ill. You have
Una	I'm not ill.
Ray	Don't come near me.
Una	I'm not ill.

She picks up a chair, hurls it at him.

I am not ill.
You are.

She picks up another.

Ray tries to stop her.

They struggle together.

Una falls to the floor, shouts out in pain.

Ray	Are you alright?
Una	Get away from me.

Pause.

Ray   How long did it take you to drive?

Una   Why?

Una   Have you driven it recently?

Una gives a short laugh.

You have
on your shirt.
It's wet.
Food or

Ray   Jesus.

Una   What is it?

Ray   I don't know.
It's wet.
Jesus.
I have to

He goes to a locker, opens it.

Nothing.
I thought there might be another shirt.

He sits down.

I'm tired.

Una   I'm tired as well.

Ray   I started at six this morning.

Una   Long day.

Ray   Double shift.

Una   You used to like good clothes.
That jacket you had.

Ray   I don't know what happened to that.

Una   Your clothes now, they're

Ray	I know.
	Cheap.
	The pay's not great here.
	They don't pay me enough for what I do.
	I should ask for more.
	I like what you're wearing.
	Pause.
Una	Where's the water?

He picks up the bottle of water, takes it to her.

She drinks.

Pause.

	I have a job.
	I work.
	Before, I travelled for a few years.
	Now I work.
	I make good money.
	Drink in moderation.
	No eating condition.
	A few friends.
	Not many.
	My flat could be bigger.
	I'm a terrible driver.
	But my car runs perfectly.
Ray	How's your mother?
	Do you see her?
Una	I've no choice.
	She sees *me*.
	She keeps a close watch.
	Still still won't trust me.
	If she knew.
	The colour her face would go.

She laughs suddenly to herself.

My mother.
She began to find me boyfriends.
To ask around.
A few years ago.
Eligible men.
Sons of friends, of neighbours.
She invited them round to the house.
We'd drink tea.
It was like the nineteenth century.
Winning my hand.
Because I
I slept with a lot of men before that.
A lot.
And when I got unhappy.
When I'd had enough
when
when I'd made my parents suffer enough
because I told them
I'd tell them in detail what I did with these men.
I stopped.

Ray   How many?

Una   You don't think I'd keep count do you?

Ray   I don't know.
You might.

Una   Eighty-three.

Ray   Do you have someone now?

Una   Yes.

Ray   He doesn't know you're here?

Una   No.
I didn't tell him.
I've *never* told him.

I didn't want to.
I liked him too much.
We're apart now.
After three years.
But I love him.
I want to love him again.
If we can.

This water.
I need a drink.
A proper drink.
My mouth's dry.

Ray   Beer.

Una   Yes.
Is that what you drink?

Ray   Sometimes yes.
Wine.
Beer would be good.
Do you want to?

Una   Go for a drink?

Ray   There's a place not far.

Una   A drink?

Ray   No.

Una   No.

Ray   My stomach.
Too much beer.
They've got good beer.

Una   European beer?

Ray   I don't know where it's from.

Una   Holland.

Ray They'll say it's from Holland but it'll be brewed
     in Newcastle.

     They laugh.

Una The ferry from Newcastle doesn't go to
     Amsterdam.

Ray I know.

     They laugh again.

Una It's a pigsty in here.

Ray They're
     They'll come back tomorrow and eat in here again
         amongst this
     and not
     because the janitor
     the
     who cleans
     is the worst.
     He does nothing.
     He reads.
     He has an office and he sits and reads and

Una Where is he?

Ray Gets ill.
     Always ill.
     Whenever he feels like it.

     He touches his shirt again.

     This is disgusting.
     It is a pigsty.

     He runs at the bin and kicks it over.

     It falls, rubbish spills out.

     He kicks the rubbish.

Una joins in.

They kick together.

The rubbish lies everywhere.

They stop, look at each other.

They start again.

He stops, out of breath, sits.

She goes nearer to him.

Una   Are you alright?

Ray   I think so.
This feels like a wound.
It's so wet.

I'm going to die at sixty.
I know I will.
I've always
some
I believe it'll happen.
Sixty.
A feeling.
I've only four years left.
Four to go.

I wondered how you'd grow up.
What you'd become.
The kind of person you'd be.
How you'd live.
To see you now.
And you to be unhappy.
And I am the cause of that.
I never wanted to hurt you.

Una   You did.

He puts his hand out, strokes her.

Ray You were lonely.
Before you met me.
When you met me.
You were alone.
You were a lonely child.
Your parents left you to yourself.
You never said it but
when I held you in my arms I could feel it.
I see now.
I thought you were strong.
You're not.
Neither am I.

They kiss.

I did think about you.
I do think about you.

Una What do you think?
Do you think about me then?

Ray Yes.
Yes, I do.
It's all I have.

Una In that room?

Ray Yes.
Touching you.
Holding you.

Una Fucking me?

Ray Yes.
Fucking you.

Una Do you masturbate?
Do you come?

Ray Yes.

They kiss.

It gets more intense.

They begin to undress each other.

They lie down.

Ray pulls away.

No.
I can't.
I can't.

Una   I want you to.

Ray   No.

Una   Why not?

Ray   I'm sorry.
I can't.

Una   Am I too old?

Outside the room, from some distance away, an adult female voice calls out.

Voice   Peter?

Ray   It's alright.

He seems not to have heard it.

Una   Did

Voice   Peter?

He stares at the door.

Una   Is it her?

Ray   Yes.

The voice calls, fainter, further away than before.

Voice   Peter, are you here?

Ray	She's at the other end of the building.
	We can
Una	What?
Ray	We have to get out.

Pause.

The sound of the door handle turning.

Una moves over to the far wall.

Ray walks towards the lockers.

The door opens and a Girl of twelve enters.

Girl	You're here.
	Peter.
	You're here.
Ray	Hello.

The Girl goes to him, puts her arms around him.

What're you doing?

Girl	We're looking for you.
	Where have you been?
Ray	I was here.
	I'm changing.

He moves away from her.

I'm busy.

Girl	What are you doing?
Ray	Look at the mess in here.
Girl	I'll help you.

She bends down to pick up the litter.

You eat too much.

She laughs to herself.

Ray   No.
Don't, darling.
Don't.

Firmer:

Drop it.

The Girl drops the litter, stares at him.

Go and find your mum.
Tell her I'm coming.
Tell her I'll see both of you at the entrance.
I'll get the car and I'll meet you at the entrance.
Wait there for me.
I'll be a few minutes.
Go.

Girl   Come with me.

Ray   I can't.

Girl   Why?

Ray   I can't yet.
I will.
Five minutes.
I have to lock all the doors.

Girl   Why can't I stay here with you?

Ray   You shouldn't even be here.
You shouldn't be in here.
It's not allowed.
You have to go now.

The Girl sees Una.

Girl   Who's she?
Peter?
Why is she there?
Why is she hiding?

Ray	She's not hiding.
Una	I'm not hiding.

The Girl moves closer to Ray.

Girl	Peter, who is she?
Ray	A friend.
Girl	Does she work here?
Ray	No.
Una	We were just talking.
Ray	And you've interrupted us.
Girl	Are you coming with us?
Una	No.
Ray	Darling
Girl	Do you know my mum?
Una	No, I don't.
Girl	What's her name?
Ray	Una.
Una	You should go now.
Ray	You should.
Girl	I want to stay with you.
Ray	Darling you can't. You have to find Mum.
Una	Go. Please. Go. You have to.

Una guides the girl out of the door.

Silence.

She's not yours?

Ray   No.
Another man.

You're not my my
I don't have to tell you everything.

Una groans.

Don't.

Una   Oh Christ

Ray   Don't.
What you're thinking.

Una   You can't.
Oh God.

Ray   No.
I could never.
Believe me.

He moves closer to her.

I take care of her.
I look after her.
I would never.

He takes hold of her, getting more insistent.

I would never do that.
I would never.
Believe me.
You have to believe me.

He stops.

Never.

He embraces her, stroking her face.

He kisses her.

She doesn't respond.

He breaks apart from her.

There's nothing I can say.

They stare at each other.

Pause.

Both of them look at the door.

Ray takes a step towards it.

Una   Wait.
You can't.

Ray   I have to.

Una   No.

Ray   I have to go to them.

Una   No.

Ray   They need me.

She goes to him, holds him.

Una   No.
You can't.
You can't go back to them.

Ray   Let me.
Let me.

Una   No.

Ray   Let me go.
Let me.
I have to.

Una   You can't.

Ray   Get off me.

        She's clinging tighter.

        He shoves her away.

        She comes back at him.

Una   Let me come with you.
        They have to know.

Ray   Get the fuck off me.

        He throws her aside.

        Una staggers backwards.

        Ray exits.

Una   Ray.

        Una runs out of the room.

        The room is empty.

        End.

Printed in the USA
CPSIA information can be obtained
at www.ICGtesting.com
LVHW091136150724
785511LV00001B/192

9 780571 233199